PHILADELPHIA
TRAVEL GUIDE
2024

Exploring Philadelphia's Rich Heritage, Culture, and Culinary Delights.

JENNIFER JAMES

TABLE OF CONTENT

MAP OF PHILADELPHIA

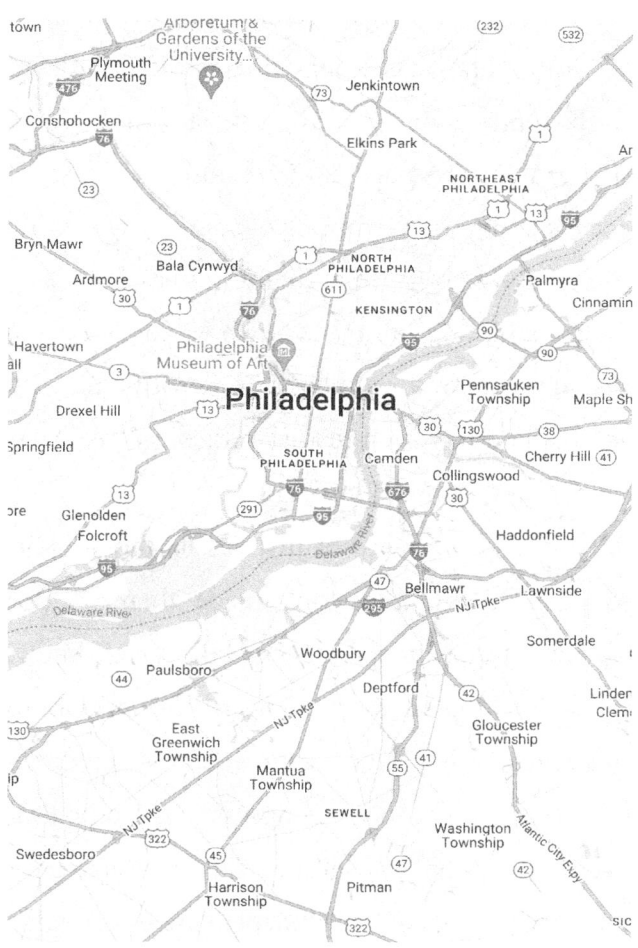

INTRODUCTION

Philadelphia is a national treasure, and the significance of its historic district is essential to the US. Philadelphia is the birthplace of several firsts in the nation; all regional advancements may be linked back to this ancient metropolis. Among many other things, Philadelphia welcomes the country's first hospital, zoo, medical school, and library. Known by most as "Philly," the state contains almost 70 National Historic Landmarks and has been recognized as a World Heritage City due to its historic significance.

The city is well-known not just for its monuments but also for the events that took place there. A popular tourist destination, Independence Hall is well-known for being the location of the signing of the Declaration of Independence. This significant location contains the Liberty Bell, the historic Congress Hall, and Franklin Court. Historians and fans alike visit its halls to get more insight into the American Independence struggle. The Edgar Allan Poe House and the Eastern State Penitentiary, a jail that has held well-known people like

Al Capone, are two other historic sites in Philadelphia. There are far too many theaters and museums in Philadelphia to mention them all, but two of the more well-known ones are the Benjamin Franklin Museum and the Philadelphia Museum of Art. Fans of motion pictures will also know that the city is home to the Rocky Statue from the "Rocky" films!

Beyond its historical monuments and buildings, Philadelphia has a lot to offer. The city is well-known throughout the country for its very recognized food, which includes sandwiches, hoagies, and the world-famous Philly Cheesesteak. For every visiting traveler, the city has several pubs and parlours, some of which date back many centuries, each with its history to uncover. Housed within the Reading Terminal structure, the Reading Terminal Market is a well-known food market that is among the biggest and most established in the world.

Philadelphia is a haven for travelers. You would need two visits to fully explore all of the city's subtleties and attractions, which would take an unfathomable amount of time.

BRIEF HISTORY

The United States was founded in Philadelphia, the nation's first World Heritage City, where our Founding Fathers gathered, spoke, argued, and eventually created a new nation.

Visitors in the twenty-first century are fortunate that so much of Philadelphia's past has survived. Naturally, this includes the two most prominent attractions in the city: the Liberty Bell, a symbol of the abolitionist cause, and Independence Hall, one of the few World Heritage sites in the nation and the location of the drafting and signing of the United States Constitution and the Declaration of Independence.

It also includes the historic homes, public buildings, museums, churches, and graveyards that comprise Independence National Historical Park, the National Parks Service's "most historic square mile in America," which welcomes millions of tourists each year.

GEOGRAPHY AND CLIMATE

On Pennsylvania's eastern border, at the meeting point of the Delaware and Schuylkill rivers, lies Philadelphia. Extremes of heat or cold are avoided because of climatic regulation provided by the Atlantic Ocean to the east and the Appalachian Mountains to the west. Now and again in the summer, the city is smothered in ocean air, which results in elevated humidity. The Schuylkill River sometimes floods due to the year-round maximum quantities of precipitation that fall throughout the summer. The northern suburbs often get more snowfall than the city, where it frequently changes to rain. Sometimes in the winter, there are strong winds.

142.71 square miles in size

Population: About 1.6 million people

Chestnut Hill, at 446 feet above sea level, is the highest point.

The sea level is the lowest point.

Philadelphia is situated on the Fall Line, which separates the Piedmont plateau area from the level Atlantic coastal plain.

It is Pennsylvania's biggest city.

The climate of Philadelphia is referred to as "humid subtropical."

Winters are quite cold, while summers are hot and muggy and autumn and spring are mild and pleasant.

TRANSPORTATION

GETTING THERE

Air Travel (Airport International of Philadelphia)

Philadelphia International Airport

In 1940, the Philadelphia International Airport was constructed. PHL is the airport's IATA code. In addition to a list of the best domestic and international flights departing from Philadelphia, Cleartrip offers details on the many airline brands that fly out of Philadelphia Airport.

From Philadelphia Airport, a variety of local and international airlines operate. Among them, United, Alaska Airlines, Sunstate Airlines / Qantaslink, and American Airlines are the airline brands that fly most often. Furthermore, with 4331 and 3467 weekly flights, respectively, the most popular routes from Philadelphia are those to Atlanta and Chicago.

The first flight out of Philadelphia airport is United Airlines flight 2246 to Minneapolis at 12:40 AM, followed at 12:50 AM by United Airlines flight 2255 to Washington. On the other hand, the last flight from

Philadelphia Airport to London, Iberia Airlines 4606, leaves at 11:15 PM

The only major airport in operation servicing the seventh-largest metropolitan region in the country is Philadelphia International Airport (PHL).

An annual total of almost 30 million passengers go through the airport.

The Airport is readily accessible via Interstates 76, 95, and 476 as well as by high-speed rail service to Center City, all of which are only seven miles from Philadelphia's downtown.

Nearly 19,000 parking spaces are available on the airport premises for both short- and long-term stays.

However, getting to and from PHL by rail and automobile is easy since there is regular public transit available, as well as access to taxi and car services.

The airport is served by SEPTA's Airport Regional Rail Line, which originates at Jefferson, 30th Street, Suburban, and University City Stations.

SEPTA's Airport Regional Rail is connected to Amtrak at William H. Gray III 30th Street Station.

Three SEPTA bus routes—Route 37 to/from South Philadelphia and Chester, Pa.; Route 108 to/from 69th Street Transportation Center; and Route 115 to/from Suburban Square in Ardmore—serve various locations around the area.

If you want to go anywhere else in the metro region, you may pay the meter ($2.70 upon admission + $2.30 for each mile). Taxis charge a fixed fee of $28.50 for travel between Center City and the airport. To get there, travelers may also grab an Uber or Lyft. For those who want to go it alone, PHL offers seven different rental vehicle companies.

PUBLIC TRANSPORTATION: (SEPTA)

Easily accessible by travelers traveling via other cities, Philadelphia is well situated between five other regional and international airports. From any of these airports, a quick rail, bus, or automobile travel will get you into Philadelphia in two hours or less:

The Southeastern Pennsylvania Transit Authority (SEPTA) serves the neighboring counties of Bucks,

Chester, Delaware, and Montgomery in addition to providing public transit into and within Philadelphia.

With rail, subway, trolley, and bus lines servicing a 2,200-square-mile area, SEPTA is the sixth-largest public transportation system in the US, providing travelers with a quick, practical, and reasonably priced option to experience Greater Philadelphia.

Seven days a week, SEPTA offers rides to Philadelphia and the Countryside as frequently as every few minutes, assisting locals and visitors in managing their daily schedules and city excursions to major events like the Philadelphia Flower Show, the city's magnificent parks, and big games at the stadium complex.

Public transit is a fantastic way to see Center City, with three main stations nearby. Some of the best places to see in Philadelphia are easily accessible by foot from Jefferson Station, Suburban Station, William H. Gray III 30th Street Station, and Philadelphia's Historic District, Reading Terminal Market, City Hall, Dilworth Park, and many more locations.

Passengers are transported to and from Philadelphia International Airport and Amtrak service by all three stops.

Subway Network

Every day, hundreds of thousands of residents and tourists travel through Philadelphia on SEPTA's subway system, which consists of the Market-Frankford Line (MFL) and the Broad Street Line (BSL).

The MFL runs east-west across the city, making stops in well-known areas including Fishtown, Old City, and University City. It is often referred to as the "blue line" due to the color of its seats and signage.

Locals refer to the line as the El, and it is elevated for a portion of the trip, providing views of the burgeoning skyline, busy commercial corridors, and the well-known Love Letters murals in West Philadelphia.

Beneath Broad Street, between North and South Philadelphia, is the BSL, or orange line. The BSL is a fantastic method for fans to travel to Eagles, Phillies, Sixers, and Flyers games as well as concerts and other events surrounding the stadium complex. NRG Station, the last station at the southern terminus of the line, is just steps away from the Wells Fargo Center and Lincoln Financial Field.

The line also passes through Olney's North Fifth Street business corridor, Center City neighborhoods like Chinatown, Logan Square, Rittenhouse Square, and Midtown Village, and North Philadelphia attractions like the renovated Met Philadelphia performing arts venue and the historic Divine Lorraine Hotel.

Buses

SEPTA customers may get ground transportation via more than 100 bus lines, which take commuters across the city and its environs and to Regional Rail stations.

The high-speed Norristown line

Parts of Delaware and Montgomery Counties are connected by SEPTA's high-speed line, which also provides access to the Market-Frankford Line subway, trolley lines, and the Manayunk/Norristown Regional Rail line.

In towns like Ardmore, where passengers may browse charming stores, have a delicious lunch, and see a comedy or music performance, the high-speed line makes a stop.

Tickets and Cash

SEPTA offers many methods for paying for a ride. Visitors can use SEPTA Key, the smart fare system, to get the best deal.

Through the Travel Wallet feature, which works like a debit card, passengers may buy and load reusable Key cards online, at SEPTA sales sites, and station kiosks.

Additionally, SEPTA offers contactless payment options for use on buses, trolleys, and both subway lines (the Broad Street Line and the Market-Frankford Line), including credit/debit cards and Apple/Google/Samsung Pay.

Subway, trolley, and bus fares are all the same. On buses and trolleys, cash or contactless payment methods are acceptable if you don't pick up a Key card.

You may also use Apple Pay, Google Pay, or Samsung Pay, your favorite smartphone payment method, or your credit or debit card to access both metro lines.

Additionally, booths on several trolley stops and metro lines sell Quick Trip single fares. On Regional Rail trains, conductors are on hand to help and may even handle onboard credit card or cash payments.

The One Day Anywhere Flex Pass, which permits up to 10 trips on SEPTA buses, trolleys, subways, and trains, is another option for travelers to explore the Philadelphia area. It can take you from Springfield to South Street, from Bensalem to the Phillies, and from Alden to the Art Museum. One may put passes directly onto a SEPTA Key Card for $13.

Availability

Wheelchair accessibility is available at several of the area's SEPTA stations, and every bus has a lift or ramp that allows it to be lowered to street level.

Operating

Recognizing the Structure of the City

Because Philadelphia is laid out in a grid, getting around is not too difficult. The principal thoroughfares that split the city into quadrants and connected to the majority of the key attractions are Broad Street and Market Street. But since the city is old, there are many one-way streets and abrupt lane changes, so you'll need to be alert and have a reliable GPS.

DRIVING AND PARKING

Driving in a city may be challenging, particularly during rush hour when the streets are alive with activity. It is necessary to pay continual attention to the presence of pedestrians, bikers, and public transit. Since drivers in Philadelphia are renowned for being aggressive, it's important to maintain awareness of your surroundings, communicate your objectives clearly, and be ready for sudden changes in traffic patterns.

Philadelphia has severe parking laws with different limits depending on the time of day and location. When parking on the street, it's usually necessary to pay at kiosks or with the meterUP app, which enables remote payments and time extensions. To prevent penalties or towing, it's essential to carefully read all signage, particularly in areas with time limitations or on days when street cleaning is taking place.

Locating a Parking Space

Street Parking: While it may be a bit of a treasure hunt to locate a place on the street in Center City, there are more options in more distant parts of the city or residential districts. Just be ready to do some walking to get there.

Parking Garages and Lots: The city is full of parking garages and lots, particularly in the vicinity of important landmarks like Independence Hall, Reading Terminal Market, and the Philadelphia Museum of Art. Though prices might vary greatly, they are often the least stressful alternative.

Parking with a Residential Permit: Certain communities need parking with a residential permit, which is not available to outsiders. Nonetheless, these locations often have sections reserved for those without permits; these areas are usually only open for two hours each day.

Advice for Easy Parking

Utilize parking apps: You can identify and book parking spots in advance, often at a reduced fee, by using apps like ParkWhiz or SpotHero. This may save a great deal of time and aggravation, particularly during events or busy periods.

If you plan to stay outside of the city or would rather not drive through Center City, you may want to think about parking near a SEPTA station and using public transit to get into the center of Philadelphia.

Be mindful of the PPA: Parking laws are strictly enforced by the Philadelphia Parking Authority (PPA). To prevent penalties or towing, pay special attention to parking signs and meter instructions.

Use Hotel Parking: A lot of hotels provide parking, either free of charge or at a cost to guests. Although sometimes more expensive than other options, this might be a handy alternative.

One is filled with anticipation as they drive into Philadelphia, seeing the city skyline rising in front of them, the iconic Liberty Bell beckoning, and the energetic streets calling. My own experience has taught me the value of readiness, patience, and the indispensable assistance of technology. It became an adventure in and of itself to navigate the city's many environments, from the busy downtown to the peaceful riverbank excursions.

BIKING AND WALKING

With more than 200 miles of bike lanes and trails, Philadelphia's growing infrastructure demonstrates the city's dedication to making it a more bike-friendly place. Visitors can easily and affordably get on a bike and tour the city thanks to the Indego Bike Share program, which makes hundreds of bikes accessible at stations across the area.

Important Bike Lanes and Trails

The Schuylkill River Trail is a multipurpose walk that runs beside the river and provides beautiful views of the Philadelphia cityscape as well as a tranquil escape from city traffic. For cyclists looking for a picturesque commute as well as those riding for fun, it's ideal.

Pine and Spruce Street Bike Lanes: These east-west lanes link several Philadelphia neighborhoods and monuments while offering a safer path through Center City.

The Circuit Trails are a massive multi-use trail network spanning over 300 miles that links the Greater Philadelphia area and provides a variety of riding experiences, from calm, woodland lanes to urban streetscapes.

Strolling about Philadelphia

One of Philadelphia's best features is that it's a highly walkable city, especially in the historic center where every step has a tale to tell. Strolling about the cobblestone alleys of Old City and the busy avenues surrounding Rittenhouse Square is a great way to gain a sense of the city's spirit, in addition to being a useful method of transportation.

Famous Paths and Places

Independence National Historical Park is a veritable gold mine for history aficionados; to understand its importance, it is best explored on foot. Home to the Liberty Bell, Independence Hall, and several other historical buildings.

Benjamin Franklin Parkway: Modeled after Paris' Champs-Élysées, this expansive boulevard links City Hall and the Philadelphia Museum of Art. It is bordered with public art, fountains, and flags, providing a charming promenade.

Rittenhouse Square: This bustling district is full of green areas, cafés, and stores where you can people-watch and take in the local way of life.

I have been able to engage with Philadelphia in ways that are not possible while seeing the city via a vehicle window, thanks to my experiences exploring the city on foot or by bicycle. My experiences have been very fulfilling because of the streets' pace, the surprising discoveries around every corner, and the palpable feeling of history. Every experience I've had seeing Philadelphia, whether it's walking the bustling streets of South Philly, taking in the peace of the Schuylkill River Trail, or feeling the cobblestones under my feet in Old City, has been a new chapter in my trip.

ACCOMMODATION

LUXURY HOTELS

1. Center City's Rittenhouse Hotel Rittenhouse Square is 100 meters away.

The Rittenhouse Hotel, which is situated in Philadelphia, provides opulent lodging along with several services, such as a parking garage, an on-site restaurant and bar, a sauna, a fitness center, a business center, and laundry facilities. In addition, the hotel offers massage treatments, a heated swimming pool, a spa, and a lovely garden. The accommodations are well-kept, roomy, and furnished, making visitors' stays pleasant. The crew makes sure that guests have a pleasant time by being amiable and providing outstanding customer service. The hotel's ideal position next to Rittenhouse Park makes it simple to go to neighboring activities and monuments. All things considered, The Rittenhouse Hotel is a great option for anyone looking for an opulent and fun place to stay in Philadelphia.

2. The Philadelphia Windsor Suites

JFK Plaza is 200 meters away from The Windsor Suites Philadelphia Center City.

For visitors on business or vacation, the Windsor Suites Philadelphia is an excellent hotel. The accommodations are roomy and well-furnished with conveniences. The hotel provides quick access to neighboring attractions and is well situated in the city core. Excellent customer service is provided by the courteous personnel and tasty meals are served in the on-site eateries. A fitness facility and an outdoor pool are among the facilities. Recommendable for its excellent location, cozy lodging, and exceptional service is The Windsor Suites Philadelphia.

3. The Franklin Institute is 400 meters away from The Logan Philadelphia, Curio Collection by Hilton Center City.

The stunning Logan Philadelphia, Curio Collection by Hilton is equipped with several features, including an indoor pool, restaurant, bar, fitness center, and spa and wellness center. The personnel is kind, accommodating, and attentive, and the rooms are well-kept and roomy, making for a nice stay. With a ton of eateries and sights close by, the location couldn't be better. The room with the pool table is one of the best features. The hotel has received great reviews from clients for both its wonderful service and the fun activities they enjoyed. Whether you're visiting the area for business or pleasure, The Logan Philadelphia is a great option for an easy and enjoyable stay.

4. Center City's Loews Philadelphia Hotel Philadelphia Marriott Downtown is 100 meters away.

The Loews Philadelphia Hotel, which is centrally located in Philadelphia, provides several facilities and services to guarantee a relaxing and pleasurable stay. For leisure, the hotel has a spa and wellness area, bar, restaurant, and exercise facility. With modern bathrooms and cozy mattresses, the rooms are tidy and well-kept. The hotel is in an ideal position, close to many well-known sites, including City Hall, the fashion area, and the Reading Terminal. The staff goes above and beyond to make customers feel welcome, and they provide exceptional service. The staff members are courteous and attentive.

All things considered, the Loews Philadelphia Hotel is a good option for a comfortable and practical stay in Philadelphia.

5. The University City Study and the Study Hotel

The Co-op restaurant's outstanding room service, immaculate amenities, and friendly personnel make The Study at University City in Philadelphia a highly recommended hotel. The rooms have lovely city views and are cozy and well-designed. It is simple to explore the city from the hotel because of its handy location close to the train station and metro. For travelers visiting Philadelphia, the hotel offers an excellent experience and is a dependable option.

BUDGET HOTELS

1. The Alexander Inn

Location: The Alexander Inn is a lovely boutique hotel in the center of Center City, putting visitors within easy walking distance of some of Philadelphia's most iconic landmarks, such as Independence Hall and the Liberty

Bell. A variety of eating and shopping alternatives are also conveniently accessible due to its central position.

Cost: Prices vary depending on the season and availability, but typically start around $120 per night.

Overview: The Alexander Inn has a warm, welcoming ambiance and vibrant art decor. Free Wi-Fi, a fitness facility, and breakfast are all available to visitors. The hotel is a great choice for those looking for affordability and character because of its distinctive design, comfy beds, and flat-screen TVs in each room.

2. The Wyndham Philadelphia Airport Microtel Inn & Suites

Location: This hotel is well situated adjacent to Philadelphia International Airport, making it a great option for transitory travelers or those wishing to stay near the airport. It provides convenient access to city exploration opportunities via public transit.

Cost: Although costs could vary depending on the season and the terms of the reservation, rates are often around $90 per night.

Overview: Ideal for early flights or late arrivals, the Microtel Inn & Suites offers contemporary, functional lodging together with free airport shuttle service. Wi-Fi, a complimentary continental breakfast, and cozy accommodations with all the conveniences are available to visitors. This motel is a sensible choice for tourists on a tight budget looking for simple, trustworthy housing.

3. Lokal Hotel Old City Location: Located in the storied Old City neighborhood, this hotel provides a special "invisible service" concept that melds the opulence of boutique lodging with the coziness of home. Notable locations include Elfreth's Alley and the Betsy Ross House, in addition to a plethora of eateries, galleries, and stores.

Cost: Considering its excellent location and the degree of comfort given, the hotel offers an inexpensive boutique experience, with rates starting at $150 a night.

Overview: The Lokal Hotel offers contemporary furniture, a fully functional kitchen, and a living space in each room to accommodate visitors who would rather stay in a more domestic setting. With computerized check-ins and an emphasis on offering a local living experience, the hotel prioritizes self-service. Travelers seeking a combination of freedom, elegance, and affordability in one of Philadelphia's most charming neighborhoods should choose this choice.

UNIQUE STAYS (B&Bs, INNS AND HOSTELS)

1. The B&B at Gables

Location: This Victorian-style bed and breakfast is tucked away in the University City district, adjacent to Drexel University and the University of Pennsylvania, providing a tranquil haven in the heart of the city.

Cost: A gourmet breakfast is included in the starting rate of around $175 per night.

Overview: With its historical charm, period furniture, wrap-around porch, and lovely garden, The Gables B&B is a standout property. Its large rooms offer guests a combination of contemporary conveniences and classic charm. The home-cooked breakfasts and the warmth of the innkeepers make this a cozy starting point for your explorations around Philadelphia.

2. Bed & Breakfast Silverstone

Situated in the charming Chestnut Hill neighborhood, this bed and breakfast provides quick access to eateries, retail stores, and the verdant Wissahickon Valley Park.

Price: Starting at $135 per night, breakfast is included.

Overview: Silverstone Bed & Breakfast is housed in a meticulously renovated 19th-century mansion and has individually designed rooms that seamlessly blend vintage charm and modern comfort. Breakfast is served to guests in the formal dining room or on the terrace outside, which has a view of a peaceful garden. It is the perfect option for anyone looking for a peaceful, picturesque stay close to the city.

INN

1. Hotel Morris House

Location: In the center of Center City, this historic boutique hotel is close to Independence Hall and Washington Square Park.

Starting at $200 per night is the cost.

Overview: Built-in 1787 and designated as a National Historic Landmark, the Morris House Hotel provides visitors with an opulent look back in time. This inn offers a distinctive fusion of comfort and history with its design from the colonial period, beautiful grounds, and contemporary conveniences. Its allure for those looking for a private, historic experience is increased by the afternoon tea service and its proximity to important sites.

2. A Hilton Hotel at The Inn at Penn

Location: This Hilton family hotel is well situated in the University City neighborhood, providing quick access to both academic and medical facilities.

Cost: The average nightly rate is around $220.

Synopsis: With chic accommodations, a cutting-edge fitness facility, and on-site eating choices, The Inn at Penn combines the allure of an old-world inn with the modern conveniences of a posh hotel. For guests seeking a mix of elegance with the kind, attentive service typical of smaller lodgings, it's ideal.

HOSTELS

1. Philadelphia's Apple Hostels

Location: This hostel is located in the Old City neighborhood, which is historically significant. It is close to Independence Hall, the Liberty Bell, and other important sites.

Cost: Private rooms are offered at a premium price, with dorm beds starting at around $40 per night.

Overview: For independent travelers and backpackers, Apple Hostels provide a lively, sociable environment. Offering an array of accommodation options, a fully functional kitchen, and a packed schedule of complementary activities and trips, it's an affordable choice without compromising on comfort or enjoyment.

2. HI Philadelphia - Mansion Chamounix

Situated in Fairmount Park, this hostel provides a calm and verdant environment at a short distance from Philadelphia's center.

Cost: The starting price for a dorm room is around $30 per night.

Synopsis: HI Philadelphia - Chamounix Mansion offers a distinctive hostel experience with both private room and dormitory alternatives, all housed in a historic mansion. Its setting in one of the biggest urban parks in the nation makes it the perfect getaway for individuals who like the outdoors and want to be close to the city's attractions without having to use public transit.

SIGHTSEEING IN PHILADELPHIA

HISTORIC LANDMARKS(LIBERTY BELL, INDEPENDENCE HALL)

There are several historic landmarks in Greater Philadelphia, but the Liberty Bell and Independence Hall, both of which are UNESCO World Heritage sites, are two of the most famous.

Whether it's your first, second, or fiftieth visit to Philadelphia, these two iconic locations—some of the most well-liked attractions in the city and some of the most well-known historic sites in the nation—must be visited.

It does need some planning to view the Bell and the Hall:

For tours to Independence Hall, guests must make reservations in advance over the phone or online.

The Liberty Bell does not now need tickets, however depending on the season, guests may have to wait in a large queue.

Independence Hall

56 delegates convened in the Pennsylvania State House in the sweltering summer of 1776, promising to spend "their lives, their fortune, and their sacred honor" to pursue independence.

The Declaration of Independence, which completed the colonies' separation from England, was signed in what is now known as Independence Hall, a UNESCO World Heritage Site.

Eleven years later, delegates from twelve states convened in the State House once more to draft the U.S. Constitution, therefore bringing the country together.

Independence Hall is a national asset that shares the status of the Statue of Liberty and Yellowstone National Park as one of only 24 World Heritage sites in the country.

How to Visit Independence Hall

The sole public access to Independence Hall is via scheduled tours (except for a few hours in January and February).

For all tours of Independence Hall, those wishing to visit between 9 a.m. and 5 p.m. must make reservations in advance.

Liberty Bell Center

The Liberty Bell doesn't ring, but its message is unmistakable: "Proclaim liberty throughout all the land unto all the inhabitants thereof."

The bell, albeit shattered, has been embraced by abolitionists, suffragists, and other advocates of freedom, partly because of its inscription.

The Liberty Bell, which was formerly displayed atop the Pennsylvania State House (now known as Independence Hall), is a well-known symbol of freedom worldwide in addition to Philadelphia.

How the Liberty Bell Center Can Be Experienced

No tickets are necessary to view the Liberty Bell. When it's busiest, visitors should prepare for a possibly lengthy wait to get in. Pro tip: Going early in the day can increase your chances of avoiding a big wait.

Expert advice:

When you leave, check the weather. There is an open space outdoors where guests wait. (Read: If there's a risk of rain, pack an umbrella.)

There aren't many spots to sit down while in line. If you can't stand for extended periods, be sure you bring a light chair or wear comfortable shoes.

MUSEUMS (PHILADELPHIA MUSEUM OF ART, THE FRANKLIN INSTITUTE)

Explore the cultural center of Philadelphia, where surprises await you around every turn. One of the most amazing collections in the nation, with some of the best examples of American, Asian, and European art anywhere, is housed in the iconic museum structure. Sunflowers by Van Gogh, the biggest Marcel Duchamp in the world, and the only dedicated Rodin Museum outside of France are all located here. Consume, hydrate, and shop. There's always something fresh to see, whether this is your first or fiftyth visit. Discover the treasures on display in the 200+ galleries of the museum, which include many breathtaking architectural spaces and historical chambers, or take in a world-class exhibition. After that, peruse the Museum Store's outstanding selection of art books and other materials, and stop by one of the cafés or Stir—the only Frank Gehry-designed restaurant on the East Coast—for a bite to eat. Children under 18 go free every time. All year long, take the family and enjoy kid-friendly programming.

Philadelphia, Pennsylvania 19130-2302; 2600 Benjamin Franklin Pkwy

222 N 20th St is the address of The Franklin Institute.

Advice: It's worth going only to see the "Giant Heart" display. Children may listen to the sounds of a real human heartbeat while climbing through the chambers of a life-like heart.

The Franklin Institute, named after the founding father and scientist Benjamin Franklin, is entertaining for guests of all ages, not just young ones. Two interactive exhibitions include "Changing Earth," where you can analyze your carbon impact, and "SportsZone," which uses simulations to illustrate the science behind rock climbing, surfing, and other sports. The Fels Planetarium allows you to explore space without leaving Earth, see 3D printers in operation, and complete a circuit with your body to light a bulb.

PARKS AND GARDENS (FAIRMOUNT PARK, SPRUCE STREET HARBOR PARK)

Since the summer of 2014, Spruce Street Harbor Park has been a Delaware River Waterfront haven, receiving quick praise as one of the greatest urban beaches in America.

During the summer, this well-liked park allows guests to play arcade games along the waterfront promenade, taste artisan beers in the beer garden, dine on floating barges and sunbathe on colorful hammocks.

The public may use the seasonal seaside park for free from May 12 to September 24, 2023. Pay as you go for both activities and concessions.

The Delaware River Waterfront Corporation created the free seasonal park at Penn's Landing, which is a must-see in Philadelphia during the summer months because of its boardwalk, brilliant LED lights, floating restaurant, beer garden, hammocks, and entertainment program.

The park is well-known for its many vibrant hammocks, which are now a certain indicator of Philly's carefree summer days.

Spruce Street Harbor Park has great outdoor activity opportunities both during the day and at night. Relaxing in a hammock or sunning by the lake are excellent reasons to come, but there's also plenty of space for lawn games and chairs, and you can hire boats (think kayaks and swan boats) at the Independence Seaport Museum, which is just next door.

Hundreds of multicolored LEDs stretched between trees in the park provide a stunning evening display as the sun sets.

Food and Drink

Spruce Street Harbor Park offers a wide variety of food and drink choices, most of which are served from stylishly renovated shipping containers that line the promenade.

This warm-weather destination offers a selection of restaurants that are representative of Philadelphia, including some of the most well-known chefs and eateries in the city. Classic Boardwalk cuisine like funnel cake and burgers are available, along with regionally developed items like cheesesteaks, Philly Taco burritos, and Chickie's and Pete's Crabfries.

For dessert, Frozen Pleasures offers, well, frozen pleasures and fried Tastykakes in the form of a carnival (yes, fried Tastykakes). French Toast Bites are back with their famous nibbles.

The Barge Bar Oasis is open daily and serves beer, wine, frozen cocktails, and more. The park's beer garden is open on weekends and has a changing range of beers.

Activities & More

Spruce Street Harbor Park offers more than just food, beverages, entertainment, and open space for relaxing; throughout the season, it also organizes weekend makers markets, outdoor dance parties, and family fun days.

Getting there

Penn's Landing, and the Delaware River Waterfront, can all be reached on foot, by bicycle, and by public transit.

You've arrived if you're walking. Go to Columbus Boulevard and Spruce Street, which is just beyond the Philadelphia Vietnam Veterans Memorial.

Take the Market-Frankford Line to 2nd Street if traveling by SEPTA, or board one of the many buses that stop at or close to Penn's Landing.

When traveling by automobile, seek parking lots along Columbus Boulevard's intersection with Lombard Circle, Walnut, and Market Streets.

The address for Fairmount Park is Reservoir Drive.

With almost 2,000 picturesque acres, Fairmount Park is the biggest manicured urban park globally, larger than Central Park in New York City. It offers chances for hiking, off-road biking (permission needed), and even equestrian riding inside the city. Additionally, picnic tables are scattered around the park and are first-come, first-served.

Fairmount Park, which is often regarded as a neighborhood in Philadelphia, is home to several well-known landmarks, such as Boathouse Row, the Philadelphia Zoo, the indoor-outdoor Mann Center, and The Philadelphia Museum of Art—some of the city's top venues for live music. Other notable sites are the Shofuso Japanese Cultural facility, which has a ceremonial tea house and koi pond, and Fairmount Water Works, which was formerly the Philadelphia Water Department's engine room but is now an event facility and a National Historic Landmark. The park stretches northwest from its starting point close to the Benjamin Franklin Parkway.

FAMILY ATTRACTIONS (PLEASE TOUCH MUSEUM, PHILADELPHIA ZOO)

The earliest and oldest zoo in the nation is the Philadelphia Zoo, which was founded in 1859 and initially opened its doors in 1874. It is also among the greatest zoos in the country because of its commitment to protecting endangered species, providing educational opportunities, and providing animal care. The Amur tiger, gigantic otter, and endangered Sumatran orangutan are among the more than 1,900 creatures that call the zoo home.

Attractions at the zoo include the kid-friendly SEPTA PZ Express Train, Wild Works Ropes Course, and Zoo360, a property-wide network of mesh paths that let animals roam across and above the zoo's grounds.

 Advice: To avoid the weekend throngs, get there early on a weekday. Even free street parking can be available to you.

The Please Touch Museum, regarded as one of the top kids' museums in the United States, provides interactive experiences for kids as young as one. You and your children may ride the priceless Woodside Park Dentzel Carousel, see Alice's Wonderland, and float boats in a water table recreation of the nearby Schuylkill River (additional costs apply). Recent visitors concur that the "Food & Family" exhibit, which has a supermarket, commercial and residential kitchens, and a community celebration space, is particularly entertaining for children.

ARTS AND CULTURE

ART GALLERIES AND INSTALLATIONS

Magic Gardens in Philadelphia

Isaiah Zagar's distinctive mosaic art environment and his public murals are preserved, interpreted, and made accessible at Philadelphia's Magic Gardens (PMG), a mosaicked visionary art environment, gallery, and community arts center. Zagar's greatest piece of art, Magic Gardens, is an expansive outdoor mosaic sculpture garden that stretches half a block down South Street in Philadelphia, as well as an entirely tiled inside area. See the two indoor galleries' constantly evolving displays from PMG inside.

1020 South Street, 19147-1936, Philadelphia, PA

Wonderspaces in Philadelphia

Wonderspaces collaborates with international artists to showcase remarkable, immersive, and thought-provoking artwork in a lighthearted, relaxed atmosphere that encourages guests to develop special bonds with friends, family, and other loved ones via uncommon shared experiences. Open all year round with a full bar within Philadelphia's Fashion District. Philadelphia, PA 19107-3004; 27 N. 11th St.

Glassworks East Falls

See free demonstrations, enroll in a class, visit a glassblowing facility, and peruse the artwork offered for sale by regional artists. The biggest hot glass gallery and workshop in Philadelphia is East Falls Glassworks. To make sure we are blowing glass that day, please give us a call before you visit. All skill levels may take classes; have a look at the Saturday Experience sessions to create your glass artwork.

19129-1566, 3510 Scotts Lane, Philadelphia, PA

THEATER AND PERFORMANCE VENUES

The Kimmel Center

The Kimmel Core for the Performing Arts, which is situated at 300 S. Broad Street in the core of Center City, is more than simply a performance space; it serves as Philadelphia's cultural hub for the performing arts. The Kimmel Center, home of the renowned Philadelphia Orchestra, presents a wide variety of events, including Broadway productions, jazz, classical music, and more. The Center is renowned for its magnificent architectural design, which includes the eye-catching Commonwealth Plaza glass dome that acts as a meeting spot for guests. The facility has many performance areas, one of which is Verizon Hall, an outstanding example of acoustical engineering.

Where: 300 S. Broad Street, Philadelphia, Pennsylvania

Opening Times: Depending on the scheduling of each performance, the box office opens at 10 AM on weekdays.

Special Features: You may take an architectural tour to learn more about the technologies and building design that go into the world-class acoustics of this structure.

2. Theater on Walnut Street

At 825 Walnut Street, the Walnut Street Theatre is the oldest continually running theater in America. Since 1809, it has led the American theatrical scene, providing audiences with a varied selection of both renowned classics and innovative new performances. The experience is further enhanced by the theatre's rich history, which included performances by notable figures like Edwin Booth and Ethel Barrymore.

Location: Philadelphia, Pennsylvania, 825 Walnut Street

Opening Times: On weekdays, box office hours are typically 10 AM to 6 PM; on performance days, these hours are extended.

Special Features: The theater provides a greater knowledge of the history and process of theater via a variety of educational programs and behind-the-scenes visits.

3. The Arden Theatre Company

The Arden Theatre Company, located at 40 N. 2nd Street in the Old City district, is well-known for its commitment to presenting outstanding narratives by outstanding storytellers. Focusing on fusing narrative with theatricality, the Arden presents a varied season of musicals and plays that include both new and old pieces. The location is renowned for its cozy atmosphere, which makes viewers feel like they are a part of the narrative.

Location: Philadelphia, PA; 40 N. 2nd Street

Opening Times: On weekdays, box office hours are normally from 10 AM to 5:30 PM; on performance days, these hours vary.

Special Features: The Arden Theatre Company offers a variety of programs designed to inspire a love of theater in young audiences. The company is devoted to education and community involvement.

LIVE MUSIC AND ENTERTAINMENT

Johnny Brenda's

Fishtown's Johnny Brenda's is a cozy, independent establishment with a fantastic view. It serves food and beverages below and stages rock, metal, and punk shows upstairs. The location has been a favorite among the community for live music events for many years.

Philadelphia, Pennsylvania 19125, USA 1201 Frankford Ave.

The Ranstead Room is a speakeasy-style cocktail bar with a brief menu of upscale beverages and small plates from El Rey. Situated on Center City's Ranstead Street, the cozy, dimly lit tavern provides an ideal ambiance for a romantic evening.

2013 Ranstead St. 19103, USA Philadelphia, PA

Bob and Barbara's Parlor

This club is well-known for its lively atmosphere, live jazz music, and inexpensive beer and shot specials. Having opened in 1969, it hosts Miss Lisa's drag performance every Thursday.

Philadelphia, PA 19146, USA 1509 South St.

Jazz Cafe Chris

Chris' Jazz Cafe, a well-liked jazz music establishment in the center of Center City, often hosts up-and-coming local and national touring bands. Every night at 8:00 p.m., there's a modest admission fee that changes according to the day of the week. Musical acts are held there.

Philadelphia, PA 19102, USA 1421 Sansom St.

World Cafe Live

University City's World Cafe Live is a great place to see independent and up-and-coming musicians perform live. It is among the top venues in Philadelphia to see a performance because of its superb acoustics. The upstairs stage is excellent for people who want more room and a longer performance, while the downstairs stage is ideal for those who prefer an intimate experience and good sightlines of the artists.

Philadelphia, PA 19104-3025 Walnut St., USA

SHOPPING AND DINING

SHOPPING DISTRICT (RITTENHOUSE SQUARE, READING TERMINAL MARKET)

Address: 18th and Walnut Streets

Reserve a table for breakfast or brunch at Parc, a French-style café with excellent cuisine, atmosphere, and people-watching.

With some of the finest restaurants, luxury shops, and cutting-edge nightlife spots in the city, this posh area is one of Philadelphia's greatest locations to dine and shop. This area of Philadelphia is also home to several of the top hotels.

Address of the Italian Market: 919 S. Ninth St.

Recommendation: Verify that Sarcone's Bakery will be open when you want to visit (and arrive early for optimal choices). Visiting the Italian Market without purchasing a couple of loaves of freshly baked bread may be considered a sin.

Visitors and residents alike agree that a trip to the Italian Market on South Ninth Street, in addition to Reading Terminal Market, is a must-do while in Philadelphia. The Italian Market is one of the nation's oldest outdoor markets, with a wide variety of gourmet food merchants offering cheeses, meats, international items, freshly roasted coffee beans, handmade chocolates, and more. Visitors like the wide selection of delectable cuisine and advice going hungry.

The address of Reading Terminal Market is 1136 Arch St.

Tasting your way around Reading Terminal Market is one of the most enjoyable (and delectable) activities you can do in Philadelphia. Over 70 merchants may be found at Reading Terminal Market, which is situated in Center City underneath the Reading Railroad's 1891 train station, which is recognized as a National Historic Landmark. Enjoy international cuisines, such as Greek, Thai, Mexican, and Indian dishes, while browsing jewelry and handcrafted items. According to recent visitors, Reading Terminal Market has something for everyone, and any queues you experience are well worth the wait.

Recommended Foods at Reading Terminal Market

It's advisable to make a list of the locations you want to visit before you enter the market since there are so many vendors there that it might seem overwhelming. Among the greatest culinary selections are:

Bakery Beiler's: Donuts

Apple dumplings in a Dutch restaurant

Cannoli from Termini Brothers Bakery; Roast Pork Sandwich from DiNic's

Saami Somi: Khachapuri, the "cheese boat" of Georgia

Getting There Parking: Hilton (11th Street and Arch Streets) and Filbert St. Parkway (12th Street & Filbert Streets) parking garages provide two-hour cheap parking. Just make a $10 minimum purchase at one of the market vendors to confirm your access. After the discount, parking will cost you around $5.

Subway: Use the Market-Frankford or Broad Street line if you're going there via subway. Nearby are the stations for 11th Street, 13th Street, and City Hall.

Bus: Reading Terminal Market is served by routes 4, 10, 11, 13, 16, 17, 21, 23, 34, 36, 38, 42, 47, and 48. The hop-on, hop-off This is also where Big Bus Philadelphia stops.

Philly Phlash: Reading Terminal Market is served by stations Nos. 4 and 20 of the Philly Phlash, a seasonal transit option to key sites.

Hours & Cost of Admission

Except on some significant holidays, Reading Terminal Market is open every day from 8 a.m. to 6 p.m., however specific merchant hours may vary. The sole expense involved in entering the market is buying goods from certain merchants.

ICONIC PHILADELPHIA FOODS

Famous Philadelphia Foods (Soft Pretzels, Cheesesteaks)

In recent decades, Philadelphia's eating sector has seen a gastronomic transformation, as new restaurants are opening up quickly around the city. The hipper Old City and Rittenhouse Square are home to the majority of the more expensive dining establishments (two relatively recent favorites are Parc, The Dandelion, and The Love). In the meantime, Center City offers delicious Japanese, Indian, and French cuisine. For straightforward Italian and farm-to-table cooking (Talula's Garden is a favorite among both reviewers and diners), go to South Philadelphia or Center City.

However, a visit to Philadelphia wouldn't be complete without trying a Philadelphia cheesesteak or a soft pretzel. The finest place to try Philly's signature sandwich, which is a hoagie-style sandwich prepared with thin slices of steak and cheese and often topped with onions, peppers, and mushrooms, is South Philly. For your personalized cheesesteak, recent visitors especially like the neighborhood's Italian Market; Pat's King of Steaks and Geno's Steaks are both well-liked destinations. An excellent location to experience an array of culinary delights is the Reading Terminal Market.

Philadelphia Cheesesteak

The cheesesteak is perhaps the most famous dish from Philadelphia. A classic cheesesteak is just a crusty bun stuffed with thinly sliced beef and your choice of cheese, such as provolone, American, or Cheez Whiz (with or without grilled onions). It was created in 1930 by Pat Olivieri of Pat's King of Steaks.

Many people travel to East Passyunk for taste-offs because of the rivalry between Pat's and Geno's Steaks, which is located across the street. Other popular steakhouses in the city include Dalessandro's Steaks and Hoagies, Joe's Steaks + Soda Shop, Steve's Prince of Steaks, Campo's Philly Cheesesteaks, and Chubby's Steaks.

Where: 600 Wendover Street, Dalessandro's Steaks

Philadelphia soft pretzel

Philadelphia soft pretzels are not like the twists you're accustomed to. They are formed like figure eight, connected in fives, and somewhat damp (so the salt melts). You'll see why Philadelphians consume 12 times as many pretzels as the typical American when you try them, however.

Street sellers, local corner shops, and bakeries such as Center City Pretzel Co., Tasty Twisters Bakery, or any of the roughly thirty Philly Pretzel Factory outlets around the city and countryside are the finest places to get pretzels. Remember to include the hot brown mustard.

Where: Several places, such as 5002 Umbria Street's Tasty Twisters Bakery

RESTAURANTS

1. Zahav

Location: Philadelphia, Pennsylvania; 237 St. James Place

Cost on average: $50 to $70 per person

Zahav, which translates as "gold" from the Hebrew, offers the golden tastes of Israel right in the middle of Philadelphia. Under the direction of James Beard Award-winning Chef Michael Solomonov, Zahav provides a contemporary Israeli dining experience that highlights the tastes of meals ranging from mezze to grilled meats with a wood-fired taboon. The restaurant has an open kitchen that lets patrons see the culinary magic in action, as well as a cozy, well-lit interior. For those who are visiting for the first time, the seasonally-changing tasting menu is highly recommended since it provides a thorough exploration of the tastes and textures that characterize Israeli cuisine.

2. Vernick Beverage & Food

Location: Philadelphia, Pennsylvania; 2031 Walnut Street

Cost on average: $60 to $90 per person

Synopsis: Located in a charming, recently renovated townhouse, Vernick Food & Drink is distinguished by its contemporary American cuisine, which blends refinement and simplicity. Another James Beard Award winner, Chef Greg Vernick, emphasizes the use of premium ingredients to create meals that are both inventive and cozy. Each area of the menu, such as "Toasts," "Raw," and "Plates," offers a variety of well-prepared foods. The atmosphere is sophisticated yet modest, ideal for large events as well as informal gatherings. Every visit to the restaurant is a smooth and delightful experience because of its dedication to providing exceptional service.

3. Roasters of coffee La Colombe

Location: Philadelphia, Pennsylvania, 1335 Frankford Avenue

Cost on average: $10 to $20 per person

More than simply a café, La Colombe is a Philadelphia success story that is renowned for its dedication to sustainable sourcing and high-quality coffee. The flagship location in Fishtown offers more than just great coffee; it's a large, industrial-chic area where guests may have light meals and pastries in addition to espresso beverages. A creamy cold-pressed espresso beverage served on tap, La Colombe's Draft Latte is a must-try.

OUTDOOR ACTIVITIES

HIKING AND BIKING TRAILS

1. Schuylkill River Trail Overview: Spanning more than 75 miles, the multipurpose trail provides paved and unpaved pathways for jogging, walking, and cycling. The route passes through some of the most attractive areas of Philadelphia, such as Center City's Schuylkill Banks, which provide breathtaking views of the city skyline.

Duration & Difficulty: The trail's difficulty varies depending on the segment. The urban portions are generally easy and flat, so hikers of all ability levels may enjoy them. Longer walks may last from half to a whole day, depending on how quickly you go and how much of the path you want to see.

Special Features: The Boardwalk, a floating boardwalk that crosses the river and provides an immersive view of the canal, is one of the trail's attractions. In addition, the route offers access to several parks and sites, such as

Valley Forge National Historical Park and the Philadelphia Museum of Art.

2. Overview of Wissahickon Valley Park's Trails: Wissahickon Valley Park, which is a part of Fairmount Park, is home to more than 50 miles of trails that wind through a breathtaking ravine covered in woods. It is a favored spot for both casual hikers and mountain bikers because of the variety of routes, which vary from simple, flat roads to more difficult rocky terrains. The Wissahickon Creek is the focal point of the park and contributes to its overall picturesque appeal.

Duration & Difficulty: Depending on the routes you pick and your speed, hiking or biking in Wissahickon Valley Park may take anything from an hour to a full day. Families and casual riders will find the broad, gravel Forbidden Drive an easy choice, while experienced hikers and cyclists may find greater obstacles on the single-track trails.

Special Features: The park's historical buildings, such as ancient mills and the Thomas Mill Covered Bridge, provide a sense of the past to your outdoor experience.

Every visit is different due to the diverse terrain, which includes vistas of creeks and lush woods.

3. John Heinz National Wildlife Refuge Trails
Overview: The John Heinz National Wildlife Refuge, which is situated near Tinicum, just outside of Philadelphia, is home to trails that meander through meadows, ponds, and forests, creating a natural paradise. Since the refuge is home to a variety of species, this is the perfect place for people wishing to combine hiking or bicycling with nature photography.

Duration & Difficulty: There are over ten miles of paths in the refuge, most of them are simple and level, making them suited for hikers of all ages and abilities. A two to three-hour excursion is ideal for a quick, revitalizing getaway into the great outdoors.

Special Features: The refuge's dedication to conservation and environmental education initiatives make it particularly noteworthy. For those who have never been here before, the Visitor Center is an excellent place to start since it offers information about the local fauna and environments. The trail's boardwalk parts provide opportunities for close-up interactions with the wetland ecosystem.

BOATING AND KAYAKING ON THE DELAWARE RIVER

There is no better way to see Philadelphia's skyline and its historic waterfronts than from the river while boating on the Delaware River. Boaters may easily set sail on a tour that blends urban discovery with the peace of river sailing, since there are multiple marinas and boat launches accessible, including the Penn's Landing Marina in the center of the city.

Access Points: With easy access to the river and other attractions, Penn's Landing is one of the most well-liked beginning locations. Many boat launch locations along the river provide a variety of boating sports, including fast boating and leisurely river excursions.

Safety and laws: To guarantee a safe trip, boaters must get acquainted with local laws, such as speed restrictions and navigation guidelines. Life jackets are mandatory, and before leaving, all boating equipment has to be inspected for safety.

Specialized Experiences: Because they provide amazing views of the city lights reflected off the lake, sunset cruises are especially well-liked. There are more reasons to cruise the Delaware River by boat during special events like riverfront concerts and fireworks shows.

Kayaking

The Delaware River offers a world of adventure for kayakers, who may explore its more populated waterfronts as well as its calmer stretches. Kayaking is a great way for both novices and expert kayakers to have a closer relationship with the water and nature.

Kayak rentals and guided trips are provided by several outfitters along the river, with tours suitable for all ability levels. These trips may improve the canoeing experience by offering a perceptive introduction to the history and ecology of the river.

Routes: Kayakers may select their own experience, from the serene waters at the John Heinz National Animal Refuge in Tinicum, which are perfect for observing local animals, to the more urban settings near the Benjamin Franklin Bridge. Paddling along the tributaries of the river, such as the Schuylkill River, adds even more variation and natural beauty.

The secret to a good kayaking excursion is planning. This includes making sure you are aware of kayaking safety procedures, dressing appropriately, and monitoring the weather and water conditions.

PUBLIC PARKS

Address of Parks Dilworth Park: 1 S. 15th St.

Dilworth Park, one of the several public parks in Philadelphia, is well-liked by both residents and visitors. This is due in part to its placement near LOVE Park and at City Hall, which is situated above Suburban Station, a major hub for public transit.

This park has features including the computer-programmable fountain known as the Albert M. Greenfield Lawn and the art project Pulse, which releases multicolored mist whenever SEPTA trains pass through the station below. On-site dining options include a restaurant, a café outside, and a Starbucks.

The address for Wissahickon Valley Park is Valley Green Road

No, driving to the mountains is not necessary to go hiking in the vicinity of Philadelphia (though it is not far from the Poconos area and all of its attractions). The 1,800-acre Wissahickon Valley Pack has more than 50 miles of hiking, mountain biking, and equestrian riding trails, and it is located about 5 miles northwest of downtown. Additionally, guests may enjoy picnics, fishing, and bird viewing along Wissahickon Creek. Visitors recommend taking a leisurely walk along the vehicle-free Forbidden Drive route to see some of the nicest vistas in the park. They also mention that on nice days, there can be crowds since it's a well-liked destination.

You'll note the park's ancient architecture as you walk about it, such as the 1737 covered bridge and the old Valley Green Inn, where you can have a bite to eat.

Rail Park Address: 1150 Callowhill St., 1300 Noble St.

This three-mile route in Philadelphia is being created from abandoned rail tracks. When everything is finished, the Rail Park will link ten communities and provide the general public with a range of facilities and regionally inspired art exhibits.

Completed Phase 1 (dubbed The Cut) has swings, bike racks, and an electric platform for events. You'll also see a variety of native Pennsylvanian flora, one of the numerous paintings around the city, and a narrative wall that portrays Philadelphia's Industrial history. There are two entrances to the existing Rail Park: Callowhill Street between 11th and 12th Streets and 1300 Noble St.

The world-famous LOVE monument by Robert Indiana, located in LOVE Park—designed by Edmund Bacon, the father of actor Kevin Bacon—is one of the most photographed locations in Philadelphia. In addition, there's a fountain that's entertaining for little children to splash around on a hot day, strolling routes, and plenty of green space.

Though they warn there's nearly always a queue, visitors agree that taking a picture in front of the LOVE sign is a must. Many tourists also recommend a visit to the nearby Philadelphia Holocaust Memorial Plaza. If you are a fan of holiday markets, plan your visit around Christmas, when the park becomes Christmas Village. This is an event that is modeled by German Christmas markets and has stunning decorations, as well as exhibitors offering handcrafted ornaments, real European cuisine, and more.

EVENTS AND FESTIVALS

MAJOR ANNUAL EVENTS

Mummers Parade

One of the oldest folk events in the country, the Mummers Parade is a New Year's Day custom that originated in Philadelphia in the 17th century. Thousands of people attend this colorful festival as Mummers, representing over 40 organized groups split into five categories: Comics, Wench Brigades, Fancies, String Bands, and Fancy Brigades. They provide lavish costumes, upbeat music, and one-of-a-kind performances that include a range of ethnic influences as they march through Philadelphia's streets.

Route and Activities: Traditionally, the procession begins in South Philadelphia, travels up Broad Street to City Hall, and concludes with the Fancy Brigade Finale at the Pennsylvania Convention Center. The sight of brilliant costumes and elaborate choreographies that use comedy, dance, and music to communicate tales is available for spectators to take in.

Experience: Being there at the Mummers Parade provides an up-close and personal peek at Philadelphia's diverse cultural landscape. Everyone who wants to kick off the new year with a celebration of creativity and community spirit may attend the event for free.

The Flower Show in Philadelphia

With more than 250,000 attendees annually, the Philadelphia Flower Exhibit, organized by the Pennsylvania Horticultural Society, is the biggest and oldest indoor flower exhibit in the world. It generally happens in March and heralds the arrival of spring by showcasing amazing flower displays and creative garden decorations. The program raises awareness of the value of green areas and environmental preservation in addition to celebrating the beauty of gardening.

Venue and Displays: Although the event has always been hosted within the Pennsylvania Convention Center, more recent iterations have taken place outside, providing a distinct atmosphere and enabling more expansive, immersive garden experiences. Every year, a new subject is introduced to the event, which directs the creation and layout of the displays, which may vary from intricate landscapes to creative flower arrangements.

Events and Learning Possibilities: The Flower Show is more than simply an artistic extravaganza; it also provides a variety of programming, such as seminars, contests, and talks by eminent authorities on design and horticulture. Families, those who love gardens, and anybody who wants to be motivated by the strength and beauty of nature should all attend.

SEASONAL FESTIVALS

Philadelphia Summer Music Festivals

The summertime in Philadelphia is filled with music because of the abundance of festivals featuring a wide range of musical styles, including jazz, rock, indie, and classical. These gatherings make use of the city's outdoor areas, providing residents and visitors with the opportunity to enjoy live music under the sky.

One of the city's most eagerly awaited summer events is the Made in America Festival, which was founded by hip-hop entrepreneur Jay-Z. This multi-genre music event, which takes place on the Benjamin Franklin Parkway during Labor Day weekend, features a variety of well-known performers as well as up-and-coming musicians on many stages. In addition to music, the festival offers a holistic cultural experience by showcasing Philadelphia's cuisine, art, and culture.

Philadelphia Folk Festival: Honoring folk, bluegrass, and world music, the Philadelphia Folk Festival is one of the nation's oldest music events. This event provides a weekend of performances, seminars, and camping in the beautiful countryside not far from the city. It's a unique way to explore the world of folk customs and inventions.

XPoNential Music Festival: Bringing together a wide array of musicians for a weekend of music on the Camden Waterfront, the festival is presented by WXPN, the University of Pennsylvania's public radio station. With its dedication to presenting up-and-coming artists alongside well-known performers, the festival has plenty to offer all types of music fans.

Philadelphia's Winter Holiday Markets

Philadelphia becomes a winter paradise when the colder months arrive, heralded by the opening of seasonal markets that infuse the city with joy and celebration. These markets, which include handcrafted goods, unusual presents, and festive food in a festively adorned environment, are ideal for Christmas shopping.

Philadelphia's Christmas Village, with its quaint wooden booths and festive lights, takes up LOVE Park and portions of City Hall. It was inspired by traditional German Christmas markets. Vendors provide a vast array of handcrafted items, ranging from jewelry and decorations to foreign delicacies and beverages. The market is a family-friendly location since it offers live entertainment and visits from Santa.

The Made in Philadelphia Holiday Market honors regional artists and craftsmen and is situated in Dilworth Park, just outside of City Hall. Enjoy the neighboring ice skating rink and winter garden, shop locally-owned stores, and purchase items with a Philadelphia theme.

Franklin Square Holiday Festival: The festival's Electrical Spectacle Holiday Light Show, which includes a gigantic kite and key modeled after Benjamin Franklin's well-known experiment, illuminates one of the city's original squares. Visitors may take advantage of seasonal cuisine, regional beers, and activities with a Christmas theme in addition to the light display.

DAY TRIPS FROM PHILADELPHIA

VALLEY FORGE NATIONAL HISTORICAL PARK

In addition to traveling through beautiful scenery, a day excursion from Philadelphia to Valley Forge National Historical Park offers an in-depth look at some of the most important periods in American history. This monument, which is about 25 miles northwest of Philadelphia, serves as a reminder of the Continental Army's valour, tenacity, and perseverance throughout the hard winter of 1777–1778. The vast grounds of the park function as a monument as well as a dynamic learning tool, giving visitors a close-up view of the setbacks and victories that helped to establish the country.

Reaching there

It takes around 30 to 45 minutes to travel from Philadelphia to Valley Forge National Historical Park, and the route is easy and picturesque. There are additional choices for public transit, such as nearby regional train services that may be completed with a quick cab or rideshare. Regardless of the means of transportation you use, the journey winds through the scenic countryside of Pennsylvania, providing the ideal backdrop for a day of discovery and introspection.

Going to Valley Forge

The Visitor Center ought to be your first visit when you arrive. A video that provides a fascinating synopsis of the historical importance of the park and the events of the winter encampment in 1777–1778 may be seen here. In addition, the center has displays and artifact exhibits that tell the Valley Forge tale concretely and provide a background for your visit.

You'll find yourself in the middle of the expansive park as soon as you exit the Visitor Center, prepared to go on a self-guided tour. A well-designated driving path inside the park goes to many important locations, including the National Memorial Arch, Washington's Headquarters, and rebuilt soldier's cottages. Every stop offers a chance to reflect on the lives of individuals who formerly tented here, the difficulties they encountered, and the tenacity with which they fought their struggles.

Trails for Biking and Walking

Valley Forge is laced with hiking and bike routes for visitors who want to get a closer look at the park's natural splendor. A well-liked option is the 5-mile Joseph Plumb Martin Trail, which leads you through the park's diverse landscapes and past several historical landmarks. Interpretive markers along the route provide details about the daily activities and strategic significance of the encampment.

Taking Stock at the Washington Headquarters

One must pay a visit to the Washington Headquarters. During the encampment, this little stone structure housed General George Washington's personal quarters and military office. Entering the same chambers that Washington used for strategy and command provides a special window into the past and a greater understanding of the difficulties faced by the nascent American military.

THE AMISH COUNTRY OF LANCASTER COUNTY

With its gentle slopes, immaculate farms, and sleepy lanes lined with horse-drawn buggies, this idyllic area beckons travelers to go back in time and see a way of life that is still closely entwined with the land and traditional traditions.

Traveling from Lancaster County to Philadelphia

Depending on traffic, the trip from Philadelphia to Lancaster County might take between one and two hours. The drive is easy and beautiful, particularly as you get closer to the county and the scenery starts to change. For those who would rather not drive, there are also scheduled excursions that leave from Philadelphia and provide escorted experiences that emphasize the Amish way of life, culture, and history.

Visiting Amish Country

The world seems to slow down considerably as you arrive, and you are greeted by a broad sky, farms, and fields. A local farm or market is a great place to start your tour of Amish Country. Sites such as The Amish

Farm and House give guided tours that provide light on everyday living, agricultural practices, and Amish customs.

Visitors may taste and buy locally produced vegetables, baked products, and handmade items at farmers' markets, including the well-known Lancaster Central Market in downtown Lancaster. These marketplaces provide witness to the Amish community's dedication to sustainability and handicrafts as well as the region's rich agricultural past.

Getting to Know the Culture

Taking a buggy ride is a great opportunity to experience the Amish way of life. Many businesses provide rides through the rural areas, allowing guests to have a better look at the tranquil beauty of the region and the chance to travel in a way that transports them back in time.

The Pennsylvanian town of Intercourse is another must-see location; it's well-known for its charming stores that provide Amish quilts, custom furniture, and other handcrafted goods. For delectable, locally created Amish delights, Bird-in-Hand's bakery and café are other reasons to come.

Eating and shopping

A visit to Lancaster County wouldn't be complete without sampling the regional food. Here, family-style eating is popular, with eateries offering filling, homemade dishes made using regional ingredients. Mainstays that provide a sense of Amish cooking customs include whoopie pies, shoofly pie, and chicken pot pie.

The region has a ton of retail stores that sell handcrafted Amish items, such as furniture, candles, and crafts, in addition to outlets. These objects are not only exquisite, but they also perfectly capture the Amish way of life with their simple design and painstaking craftsmanship.

Useful Advice for Guests

Respect for Privacy: Although the Amish community welcomes visitors, it's crucial to respect their values and right to privacy. Don't take pictures of Amish folks without their consent.

Arrange Your Visit: A lot of markets, stores, and attractions shut early or are closed on Sundays, so be sure to check their hours.

Dress Modestly: You should think about wearing modestly while visiting the Amish community as a sign of respect for their traditional beliefs.

NEW JERSEY SHORE

The Jersey Shore is the ideal vacation spot for beach lovers, families, and anybody else hoping to enjoy the sun and sea air. Its vast coastline stretches from the sandy beaches of Sandy Hook in the north to the quaint Victorian town of Cape May in the south. Depending on where you're going along the shore, the Jersey Shore is accessible and provides a range of activities to suit the interests of any tourist, all within a 1.5 to 1 hour's drive from Philadelphia.

Making Our Way to the Shore

From Philadelphia, getting to the Jersey Shore is easy; many routes take you to various locations along the shore. Whether you're traveling to Cape May, the vibrant Atlantic City, or the family-friendly Ocean City, each location has its special charm and attractions. Bus services are offered, offering direct connections to many important locations along the beach, for those who would rather not drive.

Going on the Boardwalks

No Jersey Shore vacation is complete without taking a stroll down one of the famous boardwalks. From the thrilling rides and water parks of Ocean City and Wildwood to the casinos and entertainment venues of Atlantic City, each boardwalk has its distinct personality and attractions. Shops, arcades, and restaurants line these wooden promenades, providing everything from fine seafood to traditional boardwalk fare like funnel cakes and saltwater taffy.

Relishing the Beaches

The major draw of the Jersey Shore is its kilometers of sandy beaches, which are ideal for swimming, tanning, and making sandcastles. This beach has much to offer, whether you're searching for a peaceful place to unwind or one that is packed with activity. The pristine seas and well-kept sands of the Jersey Shore beaches are well-known. Make sure to obtain a beach tag upon arrival since most beaches need them for admission throughout the summer.

Exploring Coastal Communities

Every Jersey Shore community has a distinct charm and past. History lovers and lovers of architecture should not miss Cape May, which is located at the southernmost point of New Jersey and is well-known for its Victorian architecture and historic sites. In the meanwhile, more expensive beach experiences may be found in places like Avalon and Stone Harbor, which also have great eating and boutique shopping. Asbury Park, a thriving neighborhood, is well-known for its live music culture, which includes performances by musicians like Bruce Springsteen at the storied Stone Pony.

Experimentation and Engaging Activities

There are many things to do and experiences to have at the Jersey Shore, even outside of the beach and boardwalk. Fans of water sports may go paddleboarding, kayaking, and surfing; many beaches lend out equipment for these activities. Another popular activity that gives you a chance to explore the coastline from a different angle is boat trips and fishing. The coastal nature reserves, such as the Edwin B. Forsythe National

Wildlife Refuge, provide lovely settings for nature hikes and bird viewing for those seeking a more sedate day.

PRACTICAL INFORMATION

SAFETY AND EMERGENCY SERVICES

Some of the best hospitals and medical facilities in the country are located in Philadelphia, offering both locals and tourists top-notch treatment and services. Being aware of these institutions and how to get to them might provide peace of mind in the event of a medical emergency or if you need health care services while there.

Hospitals and Emergency Services: The city is home to several well-known hospitals, including the Children's Hospital of Philadelphia (CHOP), Thomas Jefferson University Hospital, and the Hospital of the University of Pennsylvania (HUP). These facilities are prepared to treat a variety of medical conditions, from small accidents to catastrophic crises, and provide emergency services around the clock.

Urgent Care Facilities: There are several urgent care facilities in Philadelphia for non-life-threatening wounds or diseases. Seeking medical assistance from these institutions might be a more efficient and economical alternative than making an ER visit. For urgent medical needs, walk-in clinics such as MinuteClinic, AFC Urgent Care, and Vybe Urgent Care provide walk-in services.

Pharmacies: There are plenty of pharmacies in the city for prescription pharmaceuticals, over-the-counter medications, and medical supplies. Notable chains with extended hours and some 24-hour outlets include CVS, Walgreens, and Rite Aid.

Safety Advice

There are a few safety precautions to take into consideration while seeing Philadelphia guarantee a fun and safe trip:

Keep Yourself Informed: Pay attention to local news and be aware of any places that should be avoided, particularly after dark. While Center City, Old City, and the Museum District are among the city's most secure neighborhoods, it's a good idea to be vigilant and aware of your surroundings at all times.

Emergency Numbers: For prompt help in the event of an emergency, phone 911. Emergency medical services, fire, and police may be reached at this number.

Public Transportation Safety: The SEPTA buses, trolleys, and subway are just a few of the easy ways to travel about Philadelphia. But be alert, particularly at night or in less trafficked locations, and make sure your possessions are safe.

Travel Insurance: If you want to travel, you should think about getting health insurance. In the event of a medical emergency, this might provide further protection in the form of reimbursement for medical costs or emergency repatriation.

CURRENCY EXCHANGE AND BANKING

Currency Exchange: Philadelphia International Airport is a handy place to exchange currencies when you arrive. There are kiosks for exchanging currencies, such as Travelex, that provide competitive rates for a variety of currencies. Though rates in the city could be better, it's best to exchange just a modest amount at the airport.

Banks and Financial Institutions: Wells Fargo, Bank of America, PNC Bank, and other large banks are among the many Philadelphia banks that provide currency exchange services. It is advised to exchange bigger sums of money with these banks to get the greatest rates. It's a good idea to verify the policies of your bank in advance since some may demand you to have an account with them to use their currency exchange services.

Currency Exchange Offices: The city is home to many currency exchange offices, most of which are found in the tourist and retail sectors. These may be handy, but because prices and charges differ depending on where you are, it's a good idea to compare them.

Banking Services ATMs: Located all across Philadelphia, Automated Teller Machines (ATMs) provide a quick and easy method to take out cash in US dollars. Banks, convenience shops, supermarkets, and transportation hubs all have ATMs. Transaction costs should be understood since they might differ, particularly if the ATM is not run by a bank. To prevent any problems with overseas transactions, it's also a good idea to let your home bank know about your trip schedule.

Credit and Debit Cards: The majority of Philadelphia's businesses, including eateries, lodging facilities, and retail stores, accept major credit and debit cards. Commonly accepted credit cards include Visa, MasterCard, American Express, and Discover. Payments using a card might be more convenient and have better exchange rates than when using cash. It's crucial to pay attention to any overseas transaction fees that your card issuer may impose, however.

Mobile Payments: Many Philadelphia establishments now take contactless payments due to the growing use of mobile payment systems such as Apple Pay, Google Pay, and Samsung Pay. This may provide a safe and practical alternative to using cash or actual credit cards for transactions.

ITINERARIES

1-DAY HIGHLIGHTS TOUR

Morning: The National Historical Park of Independence: At the birthplace of America, get an early start to your day. See the Liberty Bell and Independence Hall, the places where the Constitution and the Declaration of Independence were discussed and decided upon. During busy hours, Independence Hall requires reservations, so make your plans in advance.

Explore Old City's cobblestone lanes, including stops at the Betsy Ross House and Elfreth's Alley, which is the oldest residential street in the country still inhabited.

In the afternoon, stop by Reading Terminal Market for lunch. There are many foreign and local cuisines available at this ancient market. Seize the opportunity to sample a traditional Philly cheesesteak.

Museum of Art in Philadelphia: Explore one of the biggest and most well-known art museums in the nation throughout the afternoon. Head up the "Rocky Steps" and take a picture with the statue of Rocky before exploring the vast array of exhibits inside the museum.

Nighttime: Rittenhouse Square Take a stroll around Rittenhouse Square, one of William Penn's five original squares, as you end your day. Savor supper at one of the numerous eateries in the vicinity, which provide a variety of options for all tastes and price ranges.

3-DAY CULTURAL EXPLORATION

First Day: Historical Perspectives

Take a deep dive into Philadelphia's rich historical basis by following the agenda of the 1-Day Highlights Tour.

Day 2: Science and Art

Morning: Take in the stunning collection of Impressionist, Post-Impressionist, and early Modern paintings at the Barnes Foundation.

In the afternoon, spend some time exploring the Franklin Institute, a top scientific museum whose mission is to ignite a curiosity in technology and science.

Evening: Take in a show at the Kimmel Center for the Performing Arts, or explore Northern Liberties' live music scene.

Day 3: Parks and Neighborhoods

Morning: Take a stroll around Fairmount Park, one of the biggest urban green areas in the nation, or start the day with a trip to the Philadelphia Zoo.

In the afternoon, take a tour of South Street's unique stores and eateries, including the Italian Market, which is the country's oldest and biggest open-air marketplace.

Evening: In Fishtown, which is well-known for its thriving culinary scene and nightlife, have a fine supper.

5 DAY FAMILY ADVENTURE

Day 3: Having Fun Outside

Morning: Get a close-up look at aquatic life by visiting the Adventure Aquarium on the Camden Waterfront.

In the afternoon, spend time at Spruce Street Harbor Park enjoying activities outside, hammock relaxation, and boardwalk-style dining.

Evening: Take the family down to Chinatown for a multi-cuisine Asian meal.

Day 4: Investigating Education

Morning: Take a look around the Please Touch Museum, which encourages play-based learning for younger kids.

Visit the Academy of Natural Sciences in the afternoon to see displays including butterflies and dinosaurs.

Evening: For a fun blend of mystery and history, take a ghost tour of old Philadelphia.

Day 5: Unwind and Have Fun

Morning: In University City, the location of Drexel University and the University of Pennsylvania, begins with a leisurely breakfast.

Afternoon: Take a stroll in the adjacent West Fairmount Park after visiting the Shofuso Japanese House and Garden.

Evening: Take a picturesque dinner cruise along the Delaware River, which offers breathtaking views of the Philadelphia cityscape, to round off your vacation.

CONCLUSION

As we conclude our journey through the pages of the "Philadelphia Travel Guide," I can't help but reflect on the incredible adventure we've shared. We've explored the rich tapestry of Philadelphia's history, soaked in the vibrant culture, and discovered the city's hidden gems.

Our journey has been more than a tourist's checklist; it's been an emotional connection to a city that embodies the spirit of freedom and resilience. From standing in the hallowed halls of Independence Hall to gazing upon timeless masterpieces at the Philadelphia Museum of Art, we've been touched by the profound stories that have unfolded before us.

Unforgettable moments abound—those quiet walks along cobblestone streets in Old City, the thrill of reaching the "Rocky Steps" at the museum, and the laughter shared over a steaming Philly cheesesteak at Reading Terminal Market.

But as we bid farewell to this guide, let me leave you with some practical tips: embrace the city's diverse neighbourhoods, savour its culinary delights, and immerse yourself in its arts and culture. Venture beyond the familiar and explore the lesser-known corners of Philadelphia, for there's always something new to discover.

I want to express my deepest gratitude for allowing me to be your guide on this journey. It's been an honor to share this experience with you, and I hope it's been as enriching for you as it has been for me.

As we part ways, remember that the world is vast, and countless adventures are waiting to be had. Let the inspiration of Philadelphia's history and spirit propel you forward to explore more of this remarkable planet we call home.

Made in the USA
Middletown, DE
05 May 2024

53909413R00066